MATH SERIES

Word Problems

Book One

by H. S. Lawrence

Book designed by Kifer Graphics

Thanks to:
Terri La Masa, Sam La Masa, Laurie Hoffman, Cody Hoffman,
and the teachers at Calahan Elementary School

Published by:
Garlic Press
100 Hillview Lane #2
Eugene, OR 97408

ISBN 0-931993-83-0
Order Number GP-083

Contents

1. Read the problem.

Read the problem. Underline what the problem is asking.

Like → this

Mike has 6 fish. His friend Pauline gave him 4 more. <u>How many total fish does Mike have now?</u>

Eddy has 6 pieces of gum. He will chew 2 pieces during lunch. How many pieces will he have left after lunch?

Mona bought shirts today. She bought 3 shirts at Mervyn's and 4 more at Walmart. How many shirts did she buy in all?

Sam has $6. Terri has $4. How much less money does Terri have than Sam?

Candy had a birthday party. Five friends came early and 7 friends came late. How many friends came altogether?

Liza and Fred went digging for seashells. Liza found 13 seashells. Fred found only 8 seashells. How many fewer seashells did Fred find than Liza?

 Susan has 5 dolls. Her sister has only 2 dolls. How many more dolls does Susan have than her sister?

 Min ate a piece of cake last night after dinner. He ate another before he went to sleep. How many pieces did he eat last night?

 A movie ticket costs $5. Billy has $8 dollars in his pocket. How much money will he have left after he buys a movie ticket?

 Marta washed 3 dishes after breakfast, another 2 after lunch, and 5 more after dinner. How many total dishes did she wash?

2. Find the facts.

Read the problem. <u>Underline what the problem is asking.</u>

Find the facts. Circle the facts that will answer the problem.

Like
this

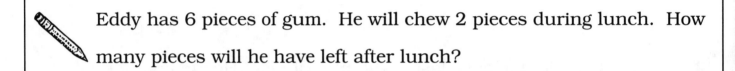

(Max had 1 bone.) His friend (Spot gave him 4 more.) How many total bones does Max have now?

Eddy has 6 pieces of gum. He will chew 2 pieces during lunch. How many pieces will he have left after lunch?

Mona bought shirts today. She bought 3 shirts at Mervyn's and 4 more at Walmart. How many shirts did she buy in all?

Sam has $6. Terri has $4. How much less money does Terri have than Sam?

Candy had a birthday party. Five friends came early and 7 friends came late. How many friends came altogether?

Liza and Fred went digging for seashells. Liza found 13 seashells. Fred found only 8 seashells. How many fewer seashells did Fred find than Liza?

 Susan has 5 dolls. Her sister has only 2 dolls. How many more dolls does Susan have than her sister?

 Min ate a piece of cake last night after dinner. He ate another before he went to sleep. How many pieces of cake did he eat last night?

 A movie ticket costs $5. Billy has $8 dollars in his pocket. How much money will he have left after he buys a movie ticket?

 Marta washed 3 dishes after breakfast, another 2 after lunch, and 5 more after dinner. How many total dishes did she wash?

3. Find the operation: Addition

Read the problem. <u>Underline what the problem is asking.</u>

Find the facts. (Circle) the facts that will answer the problem.

Find the operation. Box key words that help solve the problem.

 Like this →

(Mike has 6 fish.) (His friend Pauline gave him 4 more.) How many total fish does Mike have now?

| Key words | Key words can be helpful. Be careful! Some problems may not have key words. | | Key words for addition:
more   altogether
all   in all
total   another |  |

 Mona bought shirts today. She bought 3 shirts at Mervyn's and 4 more at Walmart. How many shirts did she buy in all?

 Candy had a birthday party. Five friends came early and 7 friends came late. How many friends came altogether?

 Marta washed 3 breakfast dishes, another 2 after lunch, and 5 more after dinner. How many total dishes did she wash?

3. Find the operation: Subtraction

Read the problem. Underline what the problem is asking.

Find the facts. (Circle) the facts that will answer the problem.

Find the operation. Box **key words that help solve the problem.**

Like this →

(Jerry bought a book for $9.00.) (Tony bought the same book) (for only $7.00.) How much less did Tony spend for the book than Jerry did?

Key words	**Key words can be helpful. Be careful! Some problems may not have key words.**	**Key words for subtraction:**
		only left
		How many fewer How much more
		How many more How much less

Eddy has 6 pieces of gum. He will chew 2 pieces during lunch. How many pieces will he have left after lunch?

Liza and Fred went digging for seashells. Liza found 13 seashells. Fred found only 8 seashells. How many fewer seashells did Fred find than Liza?

Susan has 5 dolls. Her sister has only 2 dolls. How many more dolls does Susan have than her sister?

A movie ticket costs $5. Billy has $8 dollars in his pocket. How much money will he have left after he buys a movie ticket?

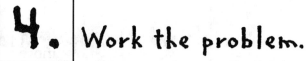

4. Work the problem.

Use the correct *facts* and the correct *operation* to work these problems. Label the answer. If you need help, use the key words on the next page.

Mike had 5 fish. His friend Pauline gave him 4 more. How many total fish does Mike have now?

Like this

$$\begin{array}{r} 5 \\ + 4 \\ \hline 9 \text{ fish} \end{array}$$

> **Fact:** Mike had 5 fish.
> **Fact:** Pauline gave him 4 more.
> **Operation:** Addition
> **Key words:** *more* and *total.*

Candy had a birthday party. Five friends came early and 7 friends came late. How many friends came altogether?

Susan has 5 dolls. Her sister has only 2 dolls. How many more dolls does Susan have than her sister?

Mona bought shirts today. She bought 3 shirts at Mervyn's and 4 more at Walmart. How many shirts did she buy in all?

Eddy has 6 pieces of gum. He will chew 2 pieces during lunch. How many pieces will he have left after lunch?

Addition Key Words:

more   altogether
all   in all
total   another

Subtraction Key Words:

only   left
How many fewer   How much more
How many more   How much less

 A movie ticket costs $5. Billy has $8 dollars in his pocket. How much money will he have left after he buys a movie ticket?

 Marta washed 3 dishes after breakfast, another 2 after lunch, and 5 more after dinner. How many total dishes did she wash?

 Liza and Fred went digging for seashells. Liza found 13 seashells. Fred found only 8 seashells. How many less seashells did Fred find than Liza?

 Sam has $6. Terri has $4. How much less money does Terri have than Sam?

 Min ate a piece of cake last night after dinner. He ate another before he went to sleep. How many pieces of cake did he eat last night?

5. Solving addition and subtraction problems.

Solve these addition and subtraction problems. Label your answers. Look for key words to help you.

Mrs. Garcia has 27 students in her class. Only 23 students came to class today. How many were absent?

The top 13 floors of an office building were damaged in a fire. The building has 25 floors. How many floors were not damaged by the fire?

Jane built a table and bench. She used 32 nails to build the table and 24 nails to build the bench. How many nails did she use in all?

Stan's scout troop is going on a pack trip. His pack weighs 22 pounds. His friend's pack weighs 34 pounds. How much more does his friend's pack weigh than his?

Elena drives a bus from town to the airport. She makes 3 stops going to the airport. She picks up 12 people at the first stop, another 12 people at the second stop, and 11 more at the last stop. How many passengers altogether arrive at the airport?

Addition Key Words:

more	altogether
all	in all
total	another

Subtraction Key Words:

only	left
How many fewer	How much more
How many more	How much less

 Fred's old ladder was 12 feet long. His new ladder is 18 feet long. How much longer is his new ladder than his old ladder?

 Miles is eating chips. He has already eaten 33 chips. If he eats another 26 chips, how may total chips will he have eaten?

 Erika must copy 75 words for homework. She has copied 42 words already. How many more words must she copy?

 Pat walks to school. She passes 13 homes on one street and 15 homes on another street. How many homes does she pass altogether?

 Two children play in the sprinklers. The sprinklers were on for 28 minutes yesterday. They were on for 16 minutes less today. How many minutes were the sprinklers on today?

11

6. Charts and graphs.

Birthdays											$\dagger$ = 1 Student
Jan	Feb	Mar	Apr	May	June	July	Aug	Sept	Oct	Nov	Dec

Mrs. Collins is a teacher. She made a chart to show how many birthdays her class would celebrate each month.

How many students are in the class?

How many more students celebrate a birthday in September than in February?

How many birthdays are in the months of June, July, and August?

These signs give directions and mileage to four towns.

Harley has stopped at the signs. He is going to visit his friend in Salem, which is 6 miles past Westridge. How many miles from the signpost is Salem?

 Mr. Wan and Mrs. DeSoto are both at the signpost. Mr. Wan is driving to Paxton. Mrs. DeSoto is driving to Eastside. How many more miles will Mrs. DeSoto drive than Mr. Wan?

 My aunt will drive from her home in Paxton to her friend's home in Westridge. She will pass the signpost on her way. How many miles is it from Paxton to Westridge?

 Westridge is on the way to Stolkid. How far is Stolkid from Westridge?

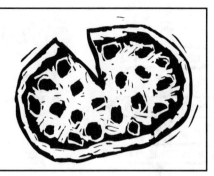

Primo Pizza

Bite a big one!

| 1 Whole Pizza | $7.00 |
| 1 Slice of Pizza | $1.00 |

 Fred, Connie, and Carol love pizza. Fred ate 2 pieces. Connie ate 1 piece. Carol had 2 pieces. How many pieces of pizza did they eat in all?

 Jackie wants to buy 2 whole pizzas. He also wants to buy 1 slice of pizza. How much will he pay altogether?

 One Primo Pizza can be cut into 8 pieces. Would it be cheaper to buy 8 pieces of pizza or a whole pizza to serve 8 people?

 Primo Pizza will deliver if you spend $9.00. What might you buy to get free delivery?

Money In The Bank

	70					70	

Aaron, Sean, Maggie, Suzanne, and Forrest all have piggy banks. The graph above shows how much each has.

How much less money does Aaron have in his bank than Sean?

Maggie and Forrest are brother and sister. They put their money together to buy a gift for their mother. How much money do they have altogether?

Suzanne wants to buy a jacket costing $55.00. How much more money does she need to buy the jacket?

15

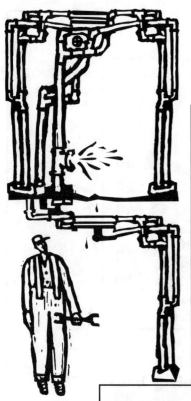

6. Finding extra information.

Sometimes word problems have more information than is needed to solve the problem.

> Paul is going to the video store. He will rent 1 action movie, 1 funny movie, and 2 scary movies. Each movie will rent for $2.00. How many total movies will Paul rent tonight?
>
> **Important facts:** He will rent 1 action movie, 1 funny movie, and 2 scary movies.
> **Extra facts:** Each movie will rent for $2.00.
> **The problem asks:** How many total movies will Paul rent tonight?

Read each problem. Circle the important facts. Draw a line through any extra information.

Paul is going to the video store. (He will rent 1 action movie,) (1 funny movie, and 2 scary movies.) ~~Each movie will rent for $2.00.~~ How many total movies will Paul rent tonight?

Jenna has 5 oranges and 3 apples. Brian has 2 oranges and 4 pears. How many more oranges does Jenna have than Brian?

Adam is a jogger. He runs 1 mile and then walks 1 mile. He then runs 2 miles back home. How many miles does he run altogether?

Lori has 3 tennis balls, 2 basketballs, and 2 tennis rackets. She also has 3 baseballs and 2 gloves. How many balls does she have altogether?

A cup on Paul's desk holds 4 pencils, 6 pens, 5 erasers, and 3 markers. How many total pens and pencils are in the cup?

 Julie, Lynn, and Sarah each have pets. Julie has 2 dogs, 1 cat, and 2 birds. Lynn has 2 cats, 2 spiders, and 1 dog. Sarah has 1 dog and 1 cat. How many more dogs does Julie have than Sarah?

 Abdul ate 3 plates of spaghetti and 3 pieces of pizza. Donald ate only 2 plates of spaghetti, but he ate 2 more pieces of pizza than Abdul did. How many pieces of pizza did Donald eat?

 Marco rode 6 rides at the county fair. He also went to the food stand 3 times to buy candy and food. There were 10 rides at the fair. How many rides did Marco not ride?

 Mary Ann read 7 books, watched 8 movies, and went to camp for 1 week. Jacob read 3 more books than Mary Ann, but he watched only 2 movies. How many books did Jacob read?

7. More problems with extra information.

Read each problem. Circle important facts. Draw a line through extra information.

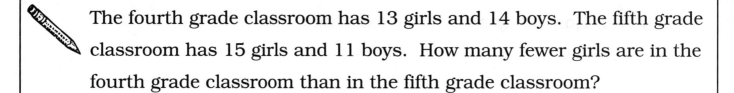

The fourth grade classroom has 13 girls and 14 boys. The fifth grade classroom has 15 girls and 11 boys. How many fewer girls are in the fourth grade classroom than in the fifth grade classroom?

Simon works at a parking lot. He parked 19 cars, 10 trucks, and 7 motorcycles yesterday. He parked 18 trucks, 12 cars, and 3 motorcycles today. How many trucks did he park in the last two days?

We gathered 17 tomatoes, 7 melons, 13 carrots, and 9 radishes today. We will cut 6 carrots for our dinner salad. How many carrots will remain after the salad is made?

The class has a set of 24 math books, 15 reading books, and 12 spelling books. How many more math books are there than spelling books?

Elena read 12 pages on Monday morning and 10 pages on Monday afternoon. She read 9 pages on Tuesday morning and 15 pages on Tuesday afternoon. How many pages did she read each morning?

The Ruiz family invited friends to their home last Sunday. Twelve people swam while 14 people watched television. Also, 7 people sat and talked. If 5 of the swimmers went to watch television. How many people watched television altogether?

Jeff's favorite candy is chocolate. He can eat a small box of 50 pieces in 2 minutes and a large box of 100 pieces in 4 minutes. If he buys a large box and eats 70 pieces, how many will be left?

Luis went to the beach Saturday morning. He counted 13 girls and 12 boys playing on the beach. He knew 5 of the boys. He counted an additional 43 girls and 31 boys later in the day. How many boys and girls did he count in all?

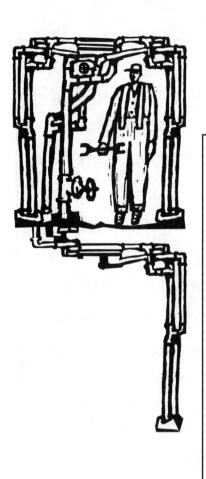

8. Solving problems with extra information.

Read the problem, find the important facts, find the operation, work the problem.

> Paul is going to the video store. He will rent 1 action movie, 1 funny movie, and 2 scary movies. Each movie will rent for $2.00. How many total movies will Paul rent tonight?
>
> **Important facts:** He will rent 1 action movie, 1 funny movie, and 2 scary movies.
> **Operation:** addition
> **Key word:** total
> **Work the problem:**
>
> $$\begin{array}{r} 1 \\ 1 \\ +\ 2 \\ \hline 4 \text{ movies} \end{array}$$

Read and solve each problem. Label your answer.

Jenna has 5 oranges and 3 apples. Brian has 2 oranges and 4 pears. How many more oranges does Jenna have than Brian?

Adam is a jogger. He runs 1 mile and then walks 1 mile. He then runs 2 miles back home. How many miles does he run altogether?

Lori has 3 tennis balls, 2 basketballs, and 2 tennis rackets. She also has 3 baseballs and 2 gloves. How many balls does she have altogether?

A cup on Paul's desk holds 4 pencils, 6 pens, 5 erasers, and 3 markers. How many total pens and pencils are in the cup?

 Julie, Lynn, and Sarah each have pets. Julie has 2 dogs, 1 cat, and 2 birds. Lynn has 2 cats, 2 spiders, and 1 dog. Sarah has 1 dog and 1 cat. How many more dogs does Julie have than Sarah?

 Abdul ate 3 plates of spaghetti and 3 pieces of pizza. Donald ate only 2 plates of spaghetti, but he ate 2 more pieces of pizza than Abdul did. How many pieces of pizza did Donald eat?

Done

 Marco rode 6 rides at the county fair. He also went to the food stand 3 times to buy candy and food. There were 10 rides at the fair. How many rides did Marco not ride?

 Mary Ann read 7 books, watched 8 movies, and went to camp for 1 week. Jacob read 3 more books than Mary Ann, but he watched only 2 movies. How many books did Jacob read?

The fourth grade classroom has 13 girls and 14 boys. The fifth grade classroom has 15 girls and 11 boys. How many fewer girls are in the fourth grade classroom than in the fifth grade classroom?

 Simon works at a parking lot. He parked 19 cars, 10 trucks, and 7 motorcycles yeaterday. He parked 18 trucks, 12 cars, and 3 motorcycles today. How many trucks did he park in the last two days?

 We gathered 17 tomatoes, 7 melons, 13 carrots, and 9 radishes today. We will cut 6 carrots for our dinner salad. How many carrots will remain after the salad is made?

 The class has a set of 24 math books, 15 reading books, and 12 spelling books. How many more math books are there than spelling books?

Elena read 12 pages on Monday morning and 10 pages on Monday afternoon. She read 9 pages on Tuesday morning and 15 pages on Tuesday afternoon. How many pages did she read each morning?

The Ruiz family invited friends to their home last Sunday. Twelve people swam while 14 people watched television. Also, 7 people sat and talked. If 5 of the swimmers went to watch television. How many people watched television altogether?

Jeff's favorite candy is chocolate. He can eat a small box of 50 pieces in 2 minutes and a large box of 100 pieces in 4 minutes. If he buys a large box and eats 70 pieces, how many will be left?

Luis went to the beach Saturday morning. He counted 13 girls and 12 boys playing on the beach. He knew 5 of the boys. He counted an additional 43 girls and 31 boys later in the day. How many boys and girls did he count in all?

More with charts and signs.

| Soup - Small Cans 54¢ | Large Cans 69¢ | 2 for $1.23 | Cup of Soup 59¢ |

Chul wants 1 small can of soup, 1 large can of soup, and 1 cup of soup. How much more will the cup of soup cost than the small can of soup?

Petra wants to buy 3 large cans of soup. She also wants to buy 2 small cans and 2 cups of soup. How much will the 2 small cans of soup cost?

Kay knows that she can buy 2 large cans of soup for a special price. She decides to buy 4 large cans. Three cans will be tomato soup and 1 can will be split pea. How much will she pay for the 4 cans at the special price?

Davie's Bakery

Cookies	Cakes	Muffins	Donuts	Bread
Oatmeal Chocolate Chip Sugar	Chocolate Lemon White	Bran Blueberry Chocolate Chip	Chocolate Plain Filled	White Wheat
35¢ each $3.50 per dozen *(1 Dozen=12)*	$5.00 (serves 6-8) $8.00 (serves 10-12)	45¢ each 3 for $1.20	45¢ each $4.50 per dozen	1 loaf $1.25 (20 slices)

 Angel wants a dozen bakery items. She wants 7 chocolate donuts and 5 filled donuts. How much will she pay?

 Tony went to the bakery and bought 1 dozen cookies and 2 loaves of bread. He ate 3 cookies immediately. How many cookies did he have for later?

 Mr. and Mrs. Chung are having a party tonight. They will buy 1 lemon cake for $8.00 and 1 chocolate cake for $5.00. They will also buy 2 muffins for their morning breakfast. How much will they pay for the two cakes?

11. Problems with several steps.

Some word problems require several steps to solve.

> Brad and Maria went to the candy store. Brad bought 2 chocolate bars and 3 suckers. Maria bought 1 candy apple and 2 jaw breakers. How many more pieces of candy did Brad buy than Maria?
>
> **What does the problem ask?** How many more pieces of candy did Brad buy than Maria?
> **What are the facts?** Brad bought 2 chocolate bars and 3 suckers. Maria bought 1 candy apple and 2 jaw breakers.

Like this →

Step 1: Add the pieces Brad bought.

$$\begin{array}{r} 2 \\ + 3 \\ \hline 5 \text{ pieces} \end{array}$$

Step 2: Add the pieces Maria bought.

$$\begin{array}{r} 1 \\ + 2 \\ \hline 3 \text{ pieces} \end{array}$$

Step 3: Subtract to find *how many more* pieces Brad bought than Maria.

$$\begin{array}{r} 5 \\ - 3 \\ \hline 2 \text{ pieces} \end{array}$$

Solve these problems. Label your answers.

Ray and Kim drew funny animals. Ray's animal had 3 front legs and 4 back legs. Kim's animal had 4 front legs and 1 back leg. How many more legs did Ray's amimal have than Amy's?

Dane bought 10 screws and 10 nails. He needed 8 of the screws and 5 of the nails to build a box. How many total screws and nails did he have left over?

 My brother had a pack of gum with 10 pieces. He gave 2 pieces to a friend and 1 piece to the friend's sister. He had 3 pieces left after he gave several pieces to our mother. How many pieces did he give our mother?

 Sam had 4 cheese sandwiches and 2 turkey sandwiches in a bag. He removed the turkey sandwiches to put in 3 more cheese sandwiches. How many total sandwiches were then in the bag?

 Cody had 5 blue marbles and 3 green marbles. He gave 2 green marbles to Nathan. He got 4 red marbles from Lois. How many marbles did he have in all?

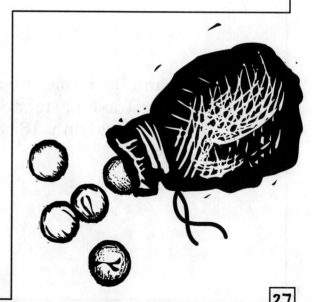

12. More problems with several steps.

Jamie picked 28 apples this morning and another 31 apples this afternoon. His mother will use 34 apples for baking. How many apples will be left over?

What does the problem ask? How many apples will be left over?

What are the facts? Jamie picked 28 apples this morning. He picked another 31 apples this afternoon.

Like this

Step 1: Add to find how many apples Jamie picked.
Key word: *another*

$$\begin{array}{r} 28 \\ +31 \\ \hline 59 \text{ apples} \end{array}$$

Step 2: Subtract the apples his mother needs to find how many will be left.

$$\begin{array}{r} 59 \\ -34 \\ \hline 25 \text{ apples} \end{array}$$

Solve these problems. Label your answers.

Larry has 24 roses for his wife. Some roses are red, some are white, and some are pink. Seven roses are pink and 4 roses are white. How many roses are red?

Peter and Rose collect empty soda pop cans. Rose collected 16 cans from one trash barrel and 13 more cans from a second barrel. Peter collected only 18 cans. How many fewer cans did Peter find than Rose?

The Park family will drive to a campground that is 97 miles from home. They will stop after 13 miles to pick up their grandmother. They will stop again after another 34 miles to shop. How many miles must the Park family still drive to the campground?

 Amelia's baseball team played a total of 27 games this season. They won their first 4 games and lost the next 5 games. They practiced hard and won the next 7 games, but then lost 4 games. They practiced even harder and won the next 6 games, but lost the final game of the season. How many more games did the team win than lose?

 A total of 58 tickets were sold to the school play last weekend. Fourteen tickets were sold Saturday morning and 23 tickets were sold Saturday evening. How many tickets were sold on Sunday?

 A.J. collects hockey cards. Her friend Louis has 89 cards. A.J. will buy 24 cards today and an additional 52 cards next week. She wants as many cards as Louis has. How many more cards does she still need?

Jake's Flower Shop

Carnations red, white, pink, yellow		Roses		Bouquets	
6 carnations	$4.49	1 dozen	$12.75	Sunshine	$14.95
1 dozen	$7.95	2 dozen	$22.98	Moonlight	$15.95
1 carnation	$ .79	1 rose	$1.25	Colorbright	$16.95
				Add 1 Balloon	$1.00

Delivery $3.00   **1 dozen=12**

Amber wants 1 dozen carnations delivered to her mother's house. Carlo wants to buy 2 dozen roses at the flower shop. How much more will Carlo pay than Amber?

Tan, Bill, and Victor want to buy a Colorbright Bouquet for their friend Ruth Ann who is sick. They also want a balloon. Tan has $5.00 and Victor has $6.50. How much will Bill need so they can get the flowers and balloon?

Pearl thinks she wants 1 Sunshine Bouquet and 6 carnations delivered to a friend's home. She changes her mind and decides to have the bouquet and 2 ballons delivered to her friend's home. How much will she pay?

Airport Shuttle Buses

 The Salinas family rode Neil's Shuttle. As they got on, 5 people were seated in the bus. How many seats were empty?

 Pam picked up 11 people at her first stop and 13 people at her second stop. Twelve people waited at the third stop. How many people at the third stop will not be able to get on the bus?

 Neil and Pam drive people to the airport. Only 1 seat is left on Neil's bus. On Pam's bus, 11 seats are left. How many more people are riding Pam's bus?

14. Post test.

Use after completing pages 4-10.

Underline what the problem is asking:

Mike saw 2 big dogs running up the street. He also saw 2 small dogs running down the street. How many total dogs did Mike see?

Underline the important facts in the problem:

Yan had 7 candles. She gave 3 candles to Lois. How many candles did she have left?

Circle the **addition** key words:

left	all	total	only	another
how many		more		altogether

Circle the **subtraction** key words:

how much less	in all	only	more
how many more	total		

Read the problem. Circle the correct operation to answer the problem.

Jim has 72 marbles. Elena has 79 marbles. How many more marbles does Elena have than Jim?

addition   subtraction

Ira has 2 pens. He is given 3 more. How many total pens does he have?

1 pen

5

5 pens

 Glen is 9 years old. His sister Jo Ann is 3 years younger. How old is Jo Ann?

6 years old

4

5 years old

 Robin picked 6 apples from an apple tree. June picked another 5 apples from the same tree. How many apples did they pick altogether?

10 apples

11 pears

11 apples

 Donna had 6 packs of crayons. Adam has 3 packs. How many fewer packs does Adam have than Donna?

2 packs

3 packs

3

 Ben has 3 models. Karen has 4 models. Lee has 2 models. How many models do they have in all?

7 models

9

9 models

Circle the important facts after reading the problem:

Two black rabbits are near a tree. Three grey rabbits, 2 white rabbits, and 2 more black rabbits soon appeared. How many total black and white rabbits are near the tree?

> 2 black rabbits are near the tree
> 2 white rabbits soon appeared
> 3 grey rabbits soon appeared
> 2 more black rabbits soon appeared

 Draw a line through the extra information in this problem:

May made a sandwich with 2 bread slices, 1 cheese slice, and 2 ham slices. Victor made a sandwich with 2 bread slices, 1 cheese slice, 2 lettuce pieces, 1 tomato slice, and 2 ham slices. How many items did May put on her sandwich?

 Zak rode his bicycle for 7 minutes. He rollerbladed for 12 minutes. His friend Mike rode his bicycle for 10 minutes. How much less time did Zak ride his bicycle than Mike?

> 3 minutes
> 4 minutes
> 4

 Juan has 3 dogs and 2 cats. Maria has only 1 cat, but 5 dogs. How many more dogs does Maria have than Juan?

> 3 dogs
> 3
> 2 dogs

 Saul sold 3 blue hats, 6 red hats, and 2 white hats yesterday. He sold 6 blue hats, 5 red hats, and 0 white hats today. How many red hats did he sell altogether?

> 8 red hats
> 11 red hats
> 9 red hats

Brad dropped 26 dog biscuits on the floor. His dog Spot ate 3 biscuits right away. Brad quickly gathered 12 biscuits. How many biscuits were left on the floor?

10 biscuits
12 biscuits
11 biscuits

Max is buying new shirts. He has 2 brown shirts, 3 white shirts, 2 blue shirts, and 3 grey shirts. He returns the brown and white shirts. He gets 2 more blue shirts. How many total shirts will he buy?

6 shirts
5 shirts
7 shirts

Tom ate 4 pancakes with strawberry syrup and 3 pancakes with maple syrup. Sandy ate 3 pancakes with blackberry syrup and 2 other pancakes with no syrup at all. How many total pancakes did Tom and Sandy eat?

11
12 pancakes
9 pancakes

Larry is tying bows for gifts he bought. He has tied 3 red bows, 4 blue bows, and 2 green bows. He has bought 19 gifts. How many more bows must he tie?

5 bows
4
6 bows

Five turtles are on land and 3 are in the water. Three turtles move into the water and 1 turtle moves onto land. How many more turtles are in the water than on land?

2 turtles
4 turtles
3

15. Answers.

Page 2-5.

Eddy has 6 pieces of gum. (He will chew 2 pieces during lunch.) How many pieces will he have left after lunch?

Mona bought shirts today. (She bought 3 shirts at Mervyn's) and (4 more at Walmart.) How many shirts did she buy in all?

(Sam has $6.) (Terri has $4.) How much less money does Terri have than Sam?

Candy had a birthday party. (Five friends came early) and (7 friends came late.) How many friends came altogether?

Liza and Fred went digging for seashells (Liza found 13 shells.) (Fred found only 8 shells.) How many fewer shells did Fred find than Liza?

(Susan has 5 dolls.) (Her sister has only 2 dolls.) How many more dolls does Susan have than her sister?

Min ate a piece of cake last night after dinner. (He ate another before he went to sleep.) How many pieces did he eat last night?

(A movie ticket costs $5.) (Billy has $8 in his pocket.) How much money will he have left after he buys a movie ticket?

(Marta washed 3 dishes after breakfast,) (another 2 after lunch,) and (5 more after dinner.) How many total dishes did she wash?

Page 6.

Mona bought shirts today. (She bought 3 shirts at Mervyn's) and (4 more at Walmart.) How many shirts did she buy in all?

Candy had a birthday party. (Five friends came early) and (7 friends came late) How many friends came altogether?

(Marta washed 3 dishes after breakfast) (another 2 after lunch,) and (5 more after dinner.) How many total dishes did she wash?

Page 7.

(Eddy has 6 pieces of gum.) (He will chew 2 pieces during lunch) How many pieces will he have left after lunch?

Liza and Fred went digging for seashells (Liza found 13 shells.) (Fred found only 8 shells.) How many fewer shells did Fred find than Liza?

(Susan has 5 dolls.) (Her sister has only 2 dolls.) How many more dolls does Susan have than her sister?

(A movie ticket costs $5.) (Billy has $8 in his pocket.) How much money will he have left after he buys a movie ticket?

Page 8.	**Page 9.**	**Page 10.**	**Page 11.**	**Page 12.**	**Page 13.**	**Page 14.**	**Page 15.**
12 friends	$3.00 left	4 students	6 feet	25 students	15 miles	5 pieces	$30 less
3 dolls	10 dishes	12 floors	59 chips	3 students	13 miles	$15	$35 altogether
7 shirts	5 shells	56 nails	33 words	6 birthdays	15 miles	Whole pizza	$20
4 pieces	$2.00 less	12 pounds	28 homes		16 miles	1 whole pizza	
	2 pieces	35 passengers	12 minutes			+ 2 slices or	
						9 slices	

Page 16.

(Jenna has 5 oranges) and 3 apples. (Brian has 2 oranges) and 4 pares. How many more oranges does Jenna have than Brian?

Adam is a jogger. (He runs 1 mile) and then walks 1 mile. (He then runs 2 miles back home.) How many miles does he run altogether?

(Lori has 3 tennis balls, 2 basketballs,) and 2 tennis rackets. (She also has 3 baseballs) and 2 gloves. How many balls does she have altogether?

Page 17.

A cup on Paul's desk holds (4 pencils, 6 pens,) 5 erasers, and 3 markers. How many total pens and pencils are in the cup?

Julie, Lynn, and Sarah each have pets. (Julie has 2 dogs,) 1 cat, and 2 birds. Lynn has 2 cats, 2 spiders, and 1 dog. (Sarah has 1 dog) and 1 cat. How many more dogs does Julie have than Sarah?

Abdul ate 3 plates of spaghetti and (3 pieces of pizza.) Donald ate only 2 plates of spagehetti, but (he ate 2 more pieces of pizza than) (Abdul did.) How many pieces of pizza did Donald eat?

(Marco rode 6 rides at the county fair.) He also went to the food stand 3 times to buy candy and food. (There were 10 rides at the fair.) How many rides did Marco not ride?

(Mary Ann read 7 books,) watched 8 movies, and went to camp for 1 week. (Jacob read 3 more books than Mary Ann,) but he watched only 2 movies. How many books did Jacob read?

Page 18.

(The fourth grade classroom has 13 girls) and ~~14 boys~~. (The fifth grade classroom has 15 girls) and ~~11 boys~~. How many fewer girls are in the fourth classroom than in the fifth grade classroom?

Simon works at a parking lot. ~~He parked 19 cars~~, (10 trucks) and ~~7 motorcycles yesterday~~. (He parked 18 trucks,) ~~12 cars, and 3 motorcycles today~~. How many trucks did he park in the last two days?

We gathered ~~17 tomatoes, 7 melons~~, (13 carrots,) and ~~9 radishes today~~. We will cut (6 carrots) for our dinner salad. How many carrots will remain after the salad is made?

(The class has a set of 24 math books,) ~~15 reading books~~, and (12 spelling books) How many more math books are there than spelling books?

Page 19.

(Elena read 12 pages on Monday morning) and ~~10 pages on Monday afternoon~~. (She read 9 pages on Tuesday morning) and ~~15 pages on Tuesday afternoon~~. How many pages did she read each morning?

The Ruiz family invited friends to their home last Sunday. ~~Twelve people swam~~ while (14 people watched televison.) Also, ~~7 people sat and talked~~. If (5 of the swimmers went to went to watch television), how many people watched television altogether?

Jeff's favorite candy is chocolate. He can eat ~~a small box of 50 pieces in 2 minutes~~ and (a large box of 100) in 4 minutes. If he buys a large box and (eats 70 pieces,) how many will be left?

Luis went to the beach Saturday morning. He counted 13 girls and 12 boys playing on the beach. He knew 5 of the boys. He counted an additional (43 girls) (and 31 boys) later in the day. How many boys and girls did he count in all?

Page 20.	**Page 21.**	**Page 22.**	**Page 23.**	**Page 24.**	**Page 25.**	**Page 26.**	**Page 27.**	**Page 28.**
3 oranges	10 pencils	2 girls	21 pages	5¢ more	$4.50	2 legs	2 screws/	13 roses
3 miles	&pens	28 trucks	19 people	$1.08	9 cookies		5 nails	11 cans
8 balls	1 dog	7 carrots	30 pieces	$2.46	$13		4 pieces	
	5 pieces of	12 math books	99 boys & girls				7 sandwiches	
	pizza						10 marbles	
	4 rides							
	10 books							

Page 29.	**Page 30.**	**Page 31.**	**Page 32.**		**Page 33.**
50 miles	$12.03 more	9 seats	How many total dogs did Mike see?		5 pens
7 more	$6.45	10 people	Yan had 7 candles. She gave 3 to Lois.		6 years old
games	$19.95	2 more people	all • total • another • more • altogether		11 apples
21 tickets			how much less • only • how many more		3 packs
13 more			subtraction		9 models
cards					

Page 34.

(2 black rabbits are near the tree)
(2 white rabbits soon appear)
(2 more black rabbits soon appeared)

~~Victor made a sandwich with 2 bread slices, 1 cheese slice, 2 lettuce pieces, 1 tomato slice, and 2 ham slices.~~

3 minutes
2 dogs
11 red hats

Page 35.

11 biscuits
7 shirts
12 pancakes
10 bows left to tie
2 turtles